Campbell's®
Simple 1-2-3
Recipes

Publications International, Ltd.

Favorite Brand Name Recipes at www.fbnr.com

Pictured on the front cover: Swiss Vegetable Bake *(page 49)*.
Pictured on the back cover: Shrimp & Corn Chowder with Sun-Dried
Tomatoes *(page 23)* and Chicken Nacho Tacos *(page 41)*.

ISBN-13: 978-1-4127-5923-6
ISBN-10: 1-4127-5923-4

Manufactured in China.

8 7 6 5 4 3 2 1

Microwave Cooking: Microwave ovens vary in wattage. Use the cooking
times as guidelines and check for doneness before adding more time.

Preparation/Cooking Times: Preparation times are based on the approxi-
mate amount of time required to assemble the recipe before cooking, baking, chilling or serving. These times include preparation steps such as
measuring, chopping and mixing. The fact that some preparations and
cooking can be done simultaneously is taken into account. Preparation of
optional ingredients and serving suggestions is not included.

Contents

Appetizers & Snacks

Layered Pizza Dip

1 cup part-skim ricotta cheese
½ cup chopped pepperoni
1 cup shredded mozzarella cheese (4 ounces)
1 cup Prego® Pasta Sauce, any variety
Pepperidge Farm® Garlic Bread, any variety, heated according to package directions **or** Pepperidge Farm® Crackers, any variety

START TO FINISH: 30 minutes

Prepping: 10 minutes
Baking: 15 minutes
Cooling: 5 minutes

1. Spread the ricotta cheese in an even layer in a 9-inch pie plate. Top with ¼ **cup** of the pepperoni and ½ **cup** mozzarella cheese. Carefully spread the pasta sauce over the cheese. Sprinkle with the remaining pepperoni and mozzarella cheese.

2. Bake at 375°F. for 15 minutes or until hot. Let cool for 5 minutes.

3. Serve with the garlic bread or crackers for dipping.

Makes: About 3 cups

Easy Substitution Tip: Substitute or add any of the following toppings for the pepperoni: Sliced pitted olives, sliced mushrooms, chopped sweet peppers **or** chopped onions.

Walnut-Cheddar Ball

2 cups shredded Cheddar
    cheese (8 ounces)
½ cup finely chopped
    walnuts
¼ cup mayonnaise
1 medium green onion,
    chopped (about
    2 tablespoons)
1 tablespoon Dijon-style
    mustard
1 teaspoon Worcestershire
    sauce
¼ cup chopped fresh
    parsley
1 tablespoon paprika
    Pepperidge Farm®
    Cracker Quartet **or**
    Cracker Trio
    Entertaining Collection
    Cracker Assortment

START TO FINISH: 2 hours 20 minutes

Prepping: 20 minutes
Refrigerating: 2 hours

1. Mix the cheese, walnuts, mayonnaise, green onion, mustard and Worcestershire in a 1½-quart bowl.

2. Mix the parsley and paprika on a piece of wax paper. Shape the cheese mixture into a ball, then roll in the parsley mixture to coat. Wrap in plastic wrap. Refrigerate for 2 hours or until firm.

3. Unwrap the cheese ball and place on a serving plate. Serve with the crackers.

Makes: 2 cups

Porcupine Meatballs

START TO FINISH: 35 minutes

Prepping: 15 minutes
Cooking: 20 minutes

1. Thoroughly mix the turkey, rice, egg, oregano, garlic powder and black pepper in a medium bowl.

2. Shape the mixture into 25 meatballs.

3. Heat the pasta sauce in a 12-inch skillet over medium-high heat. Add the meatballs in one layer. Heat to a boil. Reduce the heat to low. Cover and cook for 10 minutes or until meatballs are cooked through*.

Makes: 5 servings

The internal temperature of the meatballs should reach 160°F.

1 pound ground turkey
2 cups cooked brown **or** regular long-grain white rice
1 egg
¾ teaspoon dried oregano leaves, crushed
½ teaspoon garlic powder
¼ teaspoon ground black pepper
1 jar (1 pound 10 ounces) Prego® Traditional **or** Tomato, Basil & Garlic Pasta Sauce

Appetizers & Snacks

1 package (9.5 ounces)
   Pepperidge Farm®
   Mozzarella & Monterey
   Jack Cheese Texas
   Toast
6 tablespoons Pace®
   Refried Beans
   Pace® Chunky Salsa, any
   variety
   Sour cream (optional)
   Chopped green onions
   (optional)

Tex-Mex Toasts

START TO FINISH: 22 minutes

Prepping: 20 minutes
Baking: 2 minutes

1. Prepare the toast according to the package directions.

2. Spread **1 tablespoon** of the beans on each toast slice. Bake for 2 minutes more or until hot.

3. Top each toast slice with salsa, sour cream and green onions, if desired.

Makes: 6 servings

Cooking for a Crowd: Recipe may be doubled.

Hot Artichoke Dip

START TO FINISH: 40 minutes

Prepping: 10 minutes
Baking: 30 minutes

1. Heat the oven to 375°F. Mix the mayonnaise, sour cream, artichokes, peppers, cheese and ⅔ **cup** onions in 9-inch pie plate or 1-quart baking dish. Bake for 25 minutes or until hot.

2. Top with the remaining onions. Bake for 5 minutes more or until golden.

3. Serve with the crackers for dipping.

Makes: 3 cups

1 cup mayonnaise
1 cup sour cream
1 can (14 ounces)
   artichoke hearts,
   drained and chopped
¼ cup chopped roasted
   sweet peppers
¼ cup grated Parmesan
   cheese
1 can (2.8 ounces) French
   fried onions (1⅓ cups)
**Assorted Pepperidge
   Farm® Crackers**

Appetizers & Snacks

Salmon Bites

START TO FINISH: 15 minutes

Prepping: 15 minutes

1. Stir the mayonnaise and lemon juice in a medium bowl. Stir in the salmon.

2. Divide the tomato slices and salmon mixture among the toast slices and top with the red onion.

3. Cut the sandwiches diagonally into quarters. Serve immediately.

Makes: 16 appetizers

¼ cup lowfat mayonnaise
2 teaspoons fresh lemon juice
1 can (about 6 ounces) white **or** pink salmon, drained and flaked
1 medium tomato, cut in half and thinly sliced
4 slices Pepperidge Farm® **Very Thin Wheat or White Bread**, toasted
¼ cup very thinly sliced red onion

Appetizers & Snacks

Single-Serve
Southwest Dip Cups

START TO FINISH: 20 minutes

Prepping: 20 minutes

1. Place the foil cups on a serving platter.

2. Layer **about 1 tablespoon** each of the beans, salsa, avocado and cheese into **each** cup. Top each with a spoonful of sour cream and sprinkle with cilantro.

3. Serve with the chips for dipping.

Makes: 24 servings

24 Reynolds® Foil Baking Cups (2½-inch)
1 can (15.5 ounces) Pace® Refried Beans
2 jars (11 ounces each) Pace® Chunky Salsa
3 medium avocados, peeled and chopped (about 1½ cups)
1½ cups shredded Cheddar cheese (6 ounces)
1½ cups sour cream
½ cup chopped fresh cilantro leaves
Bite-size tortilla chips

Appetizers & Snacks

1 tablespoon vegetable oil
1 large eggplant, cut in cubes (about 8 cups)
1 Spanish onion, chopped (about 2 cups)
1 large red pepper, chopped (about 1 cup)
2 cloves garlic, minced
1 can (10¾ ounces) Campbell's® Condensed Tomato Soup
1⅓ cups water
1 teaspoon dried oregano leaves, crushed Pepperidge Farm® Cracker Quartet **or** Cracker Trio Entertaining Collection Cracker Assortment

Appetizers & Snacks

Caponata Appetizers

START TO FINISH: 1 hour

Prepping: 15 minutes
Cooking: 45 minutes

1. Heat the oil in a 6-quart saucepot over medium-high heat. Add the eggplant, onion, pepper and garlic and cook for 10 minutes or until the eggplant begins to soften.

2. Stir in the soup and water and heat the mixture to a boil. Cover and reduce the heat to low. Cook for 40 minutes more or until the vegetables are tender.

3. Stir in the oregano. Serve warm or at room temperature with the crackers.

Makes: 5 cups

Warm Spinach Dip

START TO FINISH: 25 minutes

Prepping: 10 minutes
Cooking: 15 minutes

1. Spray a 2-quart saucepan with cooking spray. Add the onion. Cook and stir until the onion is tender.

2. Stir in the spinach and flour. Gradually stir in the milk. Cook, stirring constantly, until it boils and thickens.

3. Stir in the picante sauce and cheese. Heat until the cheese melts. Season with pepper to taste. Serve with tortilla chips or vegetables for dipping.

Makes: 4 cups

Vegetable cooking spray
½ cup chopped onion
2 packages (10 ounces each) frozen chopped spinach, cooked and well drained
2 tablespoons all-purpose flour
1 cup milk
1 cup Pace® Picante Sauce
1 cup shredded part-skim mozzarella cheese
Ground black pepper

Appetizers & Snacks

Soup's On

Southwestern Chicken & White Bean Soup

1 tablespoon vegetable oil
1 pound skinless, boneless chicken breasts, cut into 1-inch pieces
1¾ cups Swanson® Chicken Broth (Regular, Natural Goodness™ **or** Certified Organic)
1 cup Pace® Chunky Salsa
3 cloves garlic, minced
2 teaspoons ground cumin
1 can (about 16 ounces) small white beans, rinsed and drained
1 cup frozen whole kernel corn
1 large onion, chopped (about 1 cup)

START TO FINISH: 8 to 10 hours 15 minutes

Prepping: 15 minutes
Cooking: 8 to 10 hours

1. Heat the oil in a 10-inch skillet over medium-high heat. Add the chicken and cook until it's well browned on all sides.

2. Mix the broth, salsa, garlic, cumin, beans, corn and onion in a 3½-quart slow cooker. Add the chicken.

3. Cover and cook on LOW for 8 to 10 hours* or until the chicken is cooked through.

Makes: 6 servings

*Or on HIGH for 4 to 5 hours

Italian Sausage and Spinach Soup

Vegetable cooking spray
½ pound sweet Italian pork sausage, cut into ¾-inch slices
4 cups Swanson® Chicken Broth (Regular, Natural Goodness™ **or** Certified Organic)
½ teaspoon dried oregano leaves, crushed
1 medium onion, chopped (about ½ cup)
1 medium carrot, sliced (about ½ cup)
2 cups coarsely chopped fresh spinach leaves

START TO FINISH: 25 minutes

Prepping: 5 minutes
Cooking: 20 minutes

1. Spray a 4-quart saucepot with cooking spray and heat over medium-high heat. Add the sausage and cook until it's well browned.

2. Add the broth, oregano, onion and carrot and heat the mixture to a boil. Cover and reduce the heat to low. Cook for 10 minutes or until the vegetables are tender.

3. Stir in the spinach and cook for 1 minute more.

Makes: 5 servings

Roasted Tomato & Barley Soup

START TO FINISH: 1 hour 15 minutes

Prepping: 10 minutes
Baking: 25 minutes
Cooking: 40 minutes

1. Heat the oven to 425°F. Drain the tomatoes, reserving the juice. Put the tomatoes, onions and garlic in a 17×11-inch roasting pan. Pour the oil over the vegetables and toss to coat. Bake for 25 minutes.

2. Put the roasted vegetables in a 3-quart saucepan. Add the reserved tomato juice, broth, celery and barley and heat to a boil. Cover and reduce the heat to low.

3. Cook for 35 minutes or until the barley is tender. Stir in the parsley.

Makes: 8 servings

1 can (28 ounces) diced tomatoes, undrained
2 large onions, diced (about 2 cups)
2 cloves garlic, minced
2 tablespoons olive oil
4 cups Swanson® Chicken Broth (Regular, Natural Goodness™ or Certified Organic)
2 stalks celery, diced (about 1 cup)
½ cup uncooked barley
2 tablespoons chopped fresh parsley

Creamy Citrus Tomato Soup with Pesto Croutons

1 can (10¾ ounces)
   Campbell's®
   Condensed Tomato
   Soup
1 cup milk
½ cup light cream **or**
   half-and-half
1 tablespoon lemon juice
6 tablespoons prepared
   pesto
6 slices French **or** Italian
   bread, ½-inch thick,
   toasted

START TO FINISH: 15 minutes

Prepping: 10 minutes
Cooking: 5 minutes

1. Stir the soup, milk, cream and lemon juice in a 2-quart saucepan. Heat the soup over medium heat until hot.

2. Spread **1 tablespoon** of the pesto on each toast slice.

3. Divide the soup among 6 serving bowls. Float a pesto crouton on each bowl of soup.

Makes: 6 servings

Soup's On

Creamy Irish Potato Soup

START TO FINISH: 35 minutes

Prepping: 10 minutes
Cooking: 25 minutes

1. Heat the butter in a 2-quart saucepan over medium-high heat. Add the green onions and celery and cook until the vegetables are tender.

2. Add the broth, water, black pepper and potatoes and heat to a boil. Cover and reduce the heat to low. Cook for 15 minutes more or until the potatoes are tender. Remove from the heat.

3. Place ½ of the broth mixture and ¾ **cup** milk into an electric blender container. Cover and blend until smooth. Pour into a medium bowl. Repeat the blending process with the remaining broth mixture and remaining milk. Return all of the puréed mixture to the saucepan and heat through. Sprinkle with the chives.

Makes: 5 servings

2 tablespoons butter
4 medium green onions,
   sliced (about ½ cup)
1 stalk celery, sliced
   (about ½ cup)
1¾ cups Swanson® Chicken
   Broth (Regular,
   Natural Goodness™ or
   Certified Organic)
½ cup water
⅛ teaspoon ground black
   pepper
3 medium potatoes
   (about 1 pound),
   sliced ¼-inch thick
1½ cups milk
   Sliced chives

Soup's On

1 jar (16 ounces) Pace®
　　Chipotle Chunky Salsa
1 cup water
2 tablespoons chili
　　powder
1 large onion, chopped
　　(about 1 cup)
2 pounds beef for stew,
　　cut into ½-inch pieces
1 can (about 19 ounces)
　　red kidney beans,
　　rinsed and drained
　　Shredded Cheddar
　　cheese (optional)
　　Sour cream (optional)

Chipotle Chili

START TO FINISH: 8 to 9 hours 15 minutes

Prepping: 15 minutes
Cooking: 8 to 9 hours

1. Stir the salsa, water, chili powder, onion, beef and beans in a 3½-quart slow cooker.

2. Cover and cook on LOW for 8 to 9 hours* or until the beef is fork-tender.

3. Serve with the cheese and sour cream, if desired.

Makes: 8 servings

Or on HIGH for 4 to 5 hours

Soup's On

Shrimp & Corn Chowder with Sun-Dried Tomatoes

START TO FINISH: 25 minutes

Prepping: 5 minutes
Cooking: 20 minutes

1. Heat the soup, half-and-half, corn and tomatoes in a 2-quart saucepan over medium heat to a boil. Cover and reduce the heat to low. Cook for 10 minutes.

2. Stir in the shrimp and chives and heat through.

3. Season to taste with black pepper.

Makes: 4 servings

Easy Substitution Tip: Substitute skim milk for the half-and-half.

1 can (10¾ ounces)
    Campbell's®
    Condensed Cream
    of Potato Soup
1½ cups half-and-half
2 cups whole kernel corn
2 tablespoons sun-dried
    tomatoes cut in strips
1 cup small **or** medium
    cooked shrimp
2 tablespoons chopped
    fresh chives
Ground black **or** ground
    red pepper

30-Minute Dishes

Southwest Salsa Chicken with Fresh Greens

1 tablespoon chili powder
1 teaspoon ground cumin
1½ pounds skinless,
    boneless chicken
    breast halves, cut
    into strips
1 tablespoon olive oil
1 cup Pace® Chunky Salsa
¼ cup water
1 bag (about 7 ounces)
    mixed salad greens
    (6 cups)

START TO FINISH: 20 minutes

Prepping: 10 minutes
Cooking: 10 minutes

1. Mix the chili powder and cumin in a shallow dish. Coat the chicken with the seasonings.

2. Heat the oil in a heavy 12-inch skillet over high heat. Add the chicken and cook until the chicken is blackened and cooked through*, stirring often. Remove the chicken and set aside.

3. Stir in the salsa and water. Cook and stir over medium heat until mixture is hot and bubbling. Divide the salad greens among 6 plates. Top each with chicken and salsa.

Makes: 6 servings

The internal temperature of the chicken should reach 160°F.

2 slices Pepperidge Farm®
    Sandwich White
    Bread, torn into pieces
⅓ cup shredded Parmesan
    cheese
1 clove garlic
½ teaspoon dried thyme
    leaves, crushed
⅛ teaspoon ground black
    pepper
2 tablespoons olive oil
8 fresh tilapia fish fillets
    (3 to 4 ounces **each**)
1 egg, beaten

Italian Fish Fillets

START TO FINISH: 20 minutes

Prepping: 10 minutes
Baking: 10 minutes

1. Place the bread, cheese, garlic, thyme and black pepper in an electric blender container. Cover and blend until fine crumbs form. Slowly add the olive oil and blend until moistened.

2. Put the fish fillets in a 17×11-inch roasting pan. Brush with the egg. Divide the bread crumb mixture evenly over the fillets.

3. Bake at 400°F. for 10 minutes or until the fish flakes easily when tested with a fork and the crumb topping is golden.

Makes: 8 servings

Easy Substitution Tip: Substitute about 2 pounds firm white fish fillets such as cod, haddock or halibut for the tilapia fillets.

Beef 'n' Bean Burritos

START TO FINISH: 15 minutes

Prepping: 5 minutes
Cooking/Baking: 10 minutes

1. Cook the beef and onion in a 10-inch skillet over medium-high heat until the beef is well browned, stirring frequently to break up meat. Pour off any fat.

2. Stir in the soup and water. Cook until the mixture is hot and bubbling.

3. Spoon **about ⅓ cup** of the beef mixture down the center of each tortilla. Top with cheese, salsa and sour cream. Fold the sides of the tortilla over the filling and then fold up the ends to enclose the filling.

Makes: 8 burritos

1 pound ground beef
1 small onion, chopped (about ¼ cup)
1 can (11.25 ounces) Campbell's® Condensed Fiesta Chili Beef Soup
¼ cup water
8 flour tortillas (8-inch), warmed
Shredded Cheddar cheese
Pace® Chunky Salsa
Sour cream

¾ cup Pace® Picante Sauce
½ cup plain yogurt
1 teaspoon lime juice
¼ teaspoon garlic powder
   or 2 cloves garlic,
   minced
1 pound boneless pork
   chops, ¾-inch thick
6 pita breads (6-inch),
   warmed
1 cup shredded lettuce
1 medium green onion,
   sliced (about
   2 tablespoons)

Grilled Pork in Pitas

START TO FINISH: 25 minutes

Prepping: 10 minutes
Grilling: 15 minutes

1. Mix **3 tablespoons** picante sauce, yogurt and lime juice. Refrigerate until ready to serve. Mix the remaining picante sauce and garlic powder in a small bowl.

2. Lightly oil the grill rack and heat the grill to medium-high. Grill the pork chops for 15 minutes or until chops are cooked through but slightly pink in center*, turning and brushing them often with the picante sauce mixture while they're grilling. Discard remaining picante sauce mixture.

3. Slice the pork into thin strips. Spoon the pork down the center of the pita. Top with the yogurt mixture, lettuce and green onion. Fold pita around filling.

Makes: 6 sandwiches

The internal temperature of the pork should reach 160°F.

Time-Saving Tip: To warm the pita breads, wrap them in a plain paper towel. Microwave on HIGH for 1 minute or until warm.

French Onion Burgers

START TO FINISH: 25 minutes

Prepping: 5 minutes
Cooking: 20 minutes

1. Shape the beef into 4 (½-inch) thick burgers.

2. Heat a 10-inch skillet over medium-high heat. Add the burgers and cook until they're well browned on both sides. Remove the burgers and set aside. Pour off any fat.

3. Stir in the soup into the skillet. Heat to a boil. Return the burgers to the skillet and reduce the heat to low. Cover and cook for 5 minutes or until the burgers are cooked through*. Top with cheese and continue cooking until the cheese melts. Serve burgers in rolls with soup mixture for dipping.

Makes: 4 burgers

*The internal temperature of the burgers should reach 160°F.

1 pound ground beef
1 can (10½ ounces)
    Campbell's®
    Condensed French
    Onion Soup
4 slices cheese
4 round hard rolls, split

2 cups Prego® Traditional
    Pasta Sauce
4 fully cooked breaded
    chicken cutlets
4 thin slices cooked ham
1 cup shredded mozzarella
    cheese (4 ounces)
2 tablespoons grated
    Parmesan cheese

Quick Chicken Parmesan

START TO FINISH: 15 minutes

Prepping: 5 minutes
Baking: 10 minutes

1. Spread **1 cup** of the pasta sauce in a 12×8×2-inch shallow baking dish.

2. Place the chicken cutlets over the sauce. Spoon ¼ **cup** of the remaining pasta sauce down the center of each cutlet. Top each with **1 slice** ham and ¼ **cup** mozzarella cheese. Sprinkle with the Parmesan cheese.

3. Bake at 425°F. for 10 minutes or until the cheese melts and the sauce is hot and bubbly.

Makes: 4 servings

Grilled Beef Steak with Sautéed Onions

START TO FINISH: 30 minutes

Prepping: 5 minutes
Cooking/Grilling: 25 minutes

1. Heat **1 tablespoon** oil in a 12-inch skillet over medium heat. Add the onions and cook until they're tender. Remove the onions from the skillet and keep warm.

2. Heat the remaining oil in the skillet. Add the steak pieces and cook until they're well browned on both sides.

3. Add the salsa and return the onions to the skillet. Cook for 3 minutes for medium-rare* or until desired doneness.

Makes: 8 servings

*The internal temperature of the steak should reach 145°F.

2 tablespoons olive oil
2 large onions, thinly sliced (about 2 cups)
2 pounds boneless beef sirloin, strip or rib steaks, cut into 8 pieces
1 jar (16 ounces) Pace® Chunky Salsa

Family Favorites

Ranchero Oven-Fried Chicken

2 cups Pepperidge Farm®
Herb Seasoned **or**
Corn Bread Stuffing,
crushed
½ cup all-purpose flour
1 can (10¾ ounces)
Campbell's®
Condensed Creamy
Ranchero Tomato
Soup
1 tablespoon water
4 pounds chicken parts
(breasts, thighs,
drumsticks)

START TO FINISH: 1 hour

Prepping: 10 minutes
Baking: 50 minutes

1. Put the crushed stuffing and flour on 2 separate plates.

2. Stir the soup and water in a shallow dish. Lightly coat the chicken with the flour. Dip the chicken into the soup mixture, then coat with the stuffing crumbs.

3. Put the chicken on a baking sheet. Bake at 400°F. for 50 minutes or until the chicken is cooked through*. Serve the chicken warm or at room temperature.

The internal temperature of the chicken parts should reach 170°F.

Makes: 8 servings

Cooking for a Crowd: Recipe may be doubled.

Make Ahead: Prepare the chicken as directed and cool for 30 minutes. Cover and refrigerate the chicken for up to 24 hours. When ready to serve, place the chicken on a baking sheet and bake at 350°F. for 30 minutes or until hot.

1 pound boneless beef
   sirloin **or** top round
   steak, ¾-inch thick, cut
   into 2-inch pieces
   Cracked black pepper
1 tablespoon vegetable oil
1 medium onion, finely
   chopped (about ½ cup)
1 can (10¾ ounces)
   Campbell's® Condensed
   Cream of Mushroom
   Soup (Regular **or**
   98% Fat Free)
½ cup water
¼ cup dry sherry (optional)
1 tablespoon tomato paste
¼ cup plain yogurt
   Hot cooked medium egg
   noodles
   Chopped fresh parsley

Beef Stroganoff

START TO FINISH: 20 minutes

Prepping: 10 minutes
Cooking: 10 minutes

1. Sprinkle the beef with the black pepper.

2. Heat the oil in a 10-inch skillet over medium-high heat. Add the beef and cook until it's well browned on all sides, stirring often. Remove the beef with a slotted spoon and set it aside.

3. Reduce the heat to medium. Add the onion. Cook and stir until the onion is tender. Stir in the soup, water, sherry, if desired, and tomato paste. Heat to a boil. Return the beef to the skillet and heat through. Remove from the heat. Stir in the yogurt. Serve over the noodles and sprinkle with the parsley.

Makes: 4 servings

Family Favorites

Creamy Chicken Bake

START TO FINISH: 40 minutes

Prepping: 10 minutes
Baking: 30 minutes

1. Place the chicken in a 13×9×2-inch shallow baking dish. Mix the soup, milk, garlic powder and mushrooms in a medium bowl and pour over the chicken.

2. Mix the cheese and bread crumbs with the butter in a small bowl and sprinkle over the soup mixture.

3. Bake at 400°F. for 30 minutes or until chicken is cooked through*. Place the chicken on a serving plate. Stir the sauce and serve with the chicken.

Makes: 6 servings

The internal temperature of the chicken should reach 160°F.

1½ **pounds skinless, boneless chicken breast halves (about 4 to 6)**
1 **can (10¾ ounces) Campbell's® Condensed Cream of Broccoli Soup (Regular or 98% Fat Free)**
⅓ **cup milk**
½ **teaspoon garlic powder**
1 **jar (4½ ounces) sliced mushrooms, drained**
¼ **cup grated Parmesan cheese**
¼ **cup dry bread crumbs**
2 **tablespoons butter, melted**

1 tablespoon olive oil
4 boneless pork chops,
    1-inch thick (about
    1¼ pounds)
1 can (10¾ ounces)
    Campbell's®
    Condensed Cream of
    Celery Soup (Regular
    or 98% Fat Free)
½ cup cranberry juice
2 tablespoons Dijon-style
    mustard
¼ teaspoon dried thyme
    leaves, crushed
¼ cup dried cranberries **or**
    cherries
    Hot cooked noodles

Cranberry Dijon Pork Chops

START TO FINISH: 55 minutes

Prepping: 10 minutes
Cooking/Baking: 45 minutes

1. Heat the oil in a 10-inch oven-safe skillet over medium-high heat. Add the pork chops and cook until the chops are well browned on both sides. Remove the pork chops and set them aside.

2. Stir in the soup, cranberry juice, mustard and thyme. Heat to a boil. Return the pork chops to the skillet and cover.

3. Bake at 350°F. for 45 minutes or until chops are cooked through but slightly pink in center*. Place the pork chops on a serving plate. Stir the cranberries into the skillet. Serve the sauce with the pork and noodles.

Makes: 4 servings

The internal temperature of the pork should reach 160°F.

Family Favorites

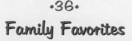

Broccoli and Pasta Bianco

START TO FINISH: 45 minutes

Prepping: 20 minutes
Baking: 25 minutes

1. Prepare the pasta according to the package directions. Add the broccoli during the last 4 minutes of the cooking time. Drain the pasta and broccoli well in a colander.

2. Stir the soup, milk and black pepper in a 12×8×2-inch shallow baking dish. Stir in the pasta mixture, ¾ **cup** of the mozzarella cheese and **2 tablespoons** of the Parmesan cheese. Top with the remaining mozzarella and Parmesan cheeses.

3. Bake at 350°F. for 25 minutes or until hot and the cheese melts.

Makes: 8 servings

1 package (16 ounces) medium tube-shaped pasta (penne)
4 cups fresh **or** frozen broccoli flowerets
1 can (10¾ ounces) Campbell's® Condensed Cream of Mushroom Soup (Regular **or** 98% Fat Free)
1½ cups milk
½ teaspoon ground black pepper
1½ cups shredded mozzarella cheese (6 ounces)
¼ cup shredded Parmesan cheese

**4 pounds pork spareribs
1 can (10¼ ounces)
Campbell's™ Beef
Gravy
¾ cup barbecue sauce
2 tablespoons packed
brown sugar**

Barbecued Pork Spareribs

START TO FINISH: 55 minutes

Prepping: 15 minutes
Cooking/Grilling: 40 minutes

1. Cut the ribs into serving pieces. Heat the ribs in a 4-quart saucepot over high heat in water to cover until the water boils. Reduce the heat to low. Cover and cook for 30 minutes until the meat is almost tender. Remove the ribs to paper towels to drain.

2. Mix the gravy, barbecue sauce and brown sugar in a large bowl. Add the ribs and toss gently to coat.

3. Lightly oil the grill rack. Preheat the grill. Grill the ribs over medium-hot coals for 10 minutes or until the meat is cooked through* and the ribs are glazed, turning the ribs over frequently during cooking and brushing with the gravy mixture occasionally.

Makes: 4 servings

*The internal temperature of the pork should reach 160°F.

Sirloin Steak Picante

START TO FINISH: 37 minutes

Prepping: 5 minutes
Grilling: 22 minutes
Standing: 10 minutes

1. Lightly oil the grill rack and heat the grill to medium. Grill the steak for 22 minutes for medium-rare* or to desired doneness, turning the steak over halfway through cooking and brushing often with **1 cup** of the picante sauce.

2. Let stand for 10 minutes before slicing.

3. Serve additional picante sauce with the steak.

Makes: 6 servings

The internal temperature of the steak should reach 145°F.

1½ pounds boneless beef sirloin or top round steak, 1½-inches thick
1 jar (16 ounces) Pace® Picante Sauce or Chunky Salsa

Family Favorites

1 can (10¾ ounces)
    Campbell's®
    Condensed Cream of
    Chicken Soup (Regular
    or 98% Fat Free)
1⅓ cups water
¾ cup **uncooked** regular
    long-grain white rice
½ teaspoon onion powder
¼ teaspoon ground black
    pepper
1½ pounds skinless,
    boneless chicken
    breast halves
    (about 4-6)
1 cup shredded Cheddar
    cheese (4 ounces)

Cheesy Chicken and Rice Bake

START TO FINISH: 50 minutes

Prepping: 5 minutes
Baking: 45 minutes

1. Mix the soup, water, rice, onion powder and black pepper in a 2-quart shallow baking dish. Top with chicken and sprinkle chicken with additional black pepper.

2. Cover and bake at 375°F. for 45 minutes or until chicken is cooked through* and rice is done.

3. Uncover and sprinkle cheese over the chicken.

Makes: 4 to 6 servings

The internal temperature of the chicken should reach 160°F.

Chicken Nacho Tacos

START TO FINISH: 25 minutes

Prepping: 10 minutes
Cooking: 15 minutes

1. Heat the oil in a 10-inch skillet over medium heat. Add the onion and chili powder and cook until the onion is tender.

2. Stir in the soup and chicken. Cook and stir until it's hot.

3. Divide the chicken mixture among the taco shells. Top with the lettuce and tomato.

Makes: 8 tacos

1 tablespoon vegetable oil
1 medium onion, chopped
   (about ½ cup)
½ teaspoon chili powder
1 can (11 ounces)
   Campbell's®
   Condensed Fiesta
   Nacho Cheese Soup
2 cans (4.5 ounces **each**)
   Swanson® Premium
   Chunk Chicken Breast,
   drained
8 taco shells **or** flour
   tortillas (6 inch),
   warmed
   Shredded lettuce **and**
   chopped tomato

Family Favorites

Holiday Fun

German Potato Salad

START TO FINISH: 1 hour 5 minutes

Prepping: 20 minutes
Cooking: 30 minutes
Cooling: 15 minutes

10 medium potatoes (about 3 pounds)
3 tablespoons chopped fresh parsley
¼ cup all-purpose flour
1¾ cups Swanson® Beef Broth (Regular, Lower Sodium **or** Certified Organic)
¼ cup cider vinegar
3 tablespoons sugar
½ teaspoon celery seed
⅛ teaspoon ground black pepper
1 medium onion, chopped (about ½ cup)

1. Put the potatoes in a 3-quart saucepan with enough water to cover them. Heat the potatoes over medium-high heat to a boil. Reduce the heat to low. Cover and cook the potatoes for 20 minutes or until they're fork-tender. Drain the potatoes well in a colander. Let cool for 15 minutes or until potatoes are cool enough to handle and cut them into cubes.

2. Mix the potatoes and parsley in a 3-quart bowl.

3. Stir the flour with the broth, vinegar, sugar, celery seed and black pepper in a 2-quart saucepan. Stir in the onion. Heat the mixture to a boil over medium-high heat. Reduce the heat to low. Cook and stir for 5 minutes or until the onion is tender and the mixture boils and thickens. Pour over the potato mixture, tossing until well coated. Serve the salad warm.

Makes: 12 servings

1 can (10¾ ounces)
    Campbell's®
    Condensed Cream of
    Mushroom Soup
    (Regular **or** 98% Fat
    Free)
½ cup milk
1 teaspoon soy sauce
    Dash ground black
    pepper
2 packages (10 ounces
    each) frozen cut
    green beans, cooked
    and drained
1 can (2.8 ounces) French
    fried onions (1⅓ cups)

Green Bean Casserole

START TO FINISH: 40 minutes

Prepping: 10 minutes
Baking: 30 minutes

1. Stir the soup, milk, soy, black pepper, green beans and ⅔ **cup** onions in a 1½-quart casserole.

2. Bake at 350°F. for 25 minutes or until hot. Stir the green bean mixture.

3. Sprinkle the remaining onions over the green bean mixture. Bake for 5 minutes more or until onions are golden brown.

Makes: 5 servings

Holiday Fun

Holiday Potato Pancakes

START TO FINISH: 55 minutes

Prepping: 25 minutes
Cooking: 30 minutes

1. Wrap the grated potatoes in a clean dish or paper towel. Twist the towel and squeeze to wring out as much of the liquid as possible.

2. Mix the soup, eggs, flour, black pepper and potatoes in a 3-quart bowl.

3. Heat ¼ **cup** oil in a deep nonstick 12-inch skillet over medium-high heat. Drop a scant ¼ **cup** potato mixture into the pan, making **4** pancakes at a time. Press on each pancake to flatten to 3 or 4 inches. Cook for 4 minutes, turning once or until the pancakes are dark golden brown. Remove the pancakes and keep warm. Repeat with the remaining potato mixture, adding more of the remaining oil as needed. Serve with the sour cream and chives.

Makes: 36 pancakes

8 medium potatoes, (about 3 pounds), peeled and grated (about 7 cups)
2 cans (10¾ ounces **each**) Campbell's® Condensed Broccoli Cheese Soup (Regular **or** 98% Fat Free)
3 eggs, beaten
2 tablespoons all-purpose flour
¼ teaspoon freshly ground black pepper
½ cup vegetable oil
Sour cream
Chopped chives

1¾ cups Swanson® Chicken Broth (Regular, Natural Goodness™ **or** Certified Organic)
3 tablespoons lemon juice
1 teaspoon dried basil leaves, crushed
1 teaspoon dried thyme leaves, crushed
⅛ teaspoon ground black pepper
12- to 14-pound turkey
2 cans (14½ ounces **each**) Campbell's™ Turkey Gravy

Holiday Fun

Herb Roasted Turkey

START TO FINISH: 4 to 4½ hours 55 minutes

Prepping: 15 minutes
Roasting: 4 to 4½ hours 30 minutes
Standing: 10 minutes

1. Mix the broth, lemon juice, basil, thyme and black pepper in a medium bowl.

2. Roast the turkey according to package directions*, basting occasionally with the broth mixture. Let the turkey stand for 10 minutes before slicing. Discard any remaining broth mixture.

3. Heat the gravy and serve with the turkey.

Makes: 12 to 14 servings

The internal temperature of the turkey should reach 180°F.

Heavenly Sweet Potatoes

START TO FINISH: 30 minutes

Prepping: 10 minutes
Baking: 20 minutes

1. Spray a 1½-quart casserole with cooking spray. Set the dish aside.

2. Place the potatoes, cinnamon and ginger in a 3-quart bowl. Beat with an electric mixer on medium speed until the potatoes are fluffy and almost smooth. Add the broth and beat until the ingredients are mixed. Spoon the potato mixture into the prepared dish. Top with the marshmallows.

3. Bake at 350°F. for 20 minutes or until hot and marshmallows are golden brown.

Makes: 8 servings

Vegetable cooking spray
1 can (40 ounces) cut sweet potatoes in heavy syrup, drained
¼ teaspoon ground cinnamon
⅛ teaspoon ground ginger
¾ cup Swanson® Chicken Broth (Regular, Natural Goodness™ or Certified Organic)
2 cups miniature marshmallows

Layered Cranberry Walnut Stuffing

**2 boxes (6 ounces each)
    Pepperidge Farm®
    Stuffing Mix**
**1½ cups Swanson® Chicken
    Broth (Regular,
    Natural Goodness™
    or Certified Organic)**
2 tablespoons butter
**1 can (16 ounces) whole
    cranberry sauce**
**½ cup walnuts, toasted
    and chopped**

START TO FINISH: 35 minutes

Prepping: 10 minutes
Baking: 25 minutes

1. Prepare the stuffing using the broth and butter according to the package directions.

2. Spoon **half** of the stuffing into a 2-quart casserole. Spoon **half** of the cranberry sauce over the stuffing. Sprinkle with ¼ **cup** walnuts. Repeat the layers.

3. Bake at 350°F. for 25 minutes or until hot.

Makes: 6 servings

Swiss Vegetable Bake

START TO FINISH: 50 minutes

Prepping: 5 minutes
Baking: 45 minutes

1. Stir the soup, sour cream, black pepper, vegetables, **1½ cups** cheese and **1⅓ cups** onions in a 13×9×2-inch shallow baking dish and cover.

2. Bake at 350°F. for 40 minutes or until the vegetables are tender. Stir the vegetable mixture.

3. Sprinkle the remaining cheese and onions over the vegetable mixture. Bake for 5 minutes more or until the onions are golden brown.

Makes: 8 servings

Time-Saving Tip: To thaw the vegetables, cut off 1 corner on bag, microwave on HIGH for 5 minutes.

1 can (26 ounces) Campbell's® Condensed Cream of Chicken Soup
⅔ cup sour cream
½ teaspoon ground black pepper
2 bags (16 ounces **each**) frozen vegetable combination (broccoli, cauliflower, carrots), thawed
2 cups shredded Swiss cheese (8 ounces)
1 can (6 ounces) French fried onions (2⅔ cups)

Holiday Fun

Vegetable cooking spray
1 jar (1 pound
    11.5 ounces) Prego®
    Hearty Meat™ Italian
    Sausage Meat Sauce
1 container (15 ounces)
    part-skim ricotta
    cheese
¾ cup grated Parmesan
    cheese
7 cups bow tie-shaped
    pasta, cooked and
    drained
1 container (8 ounces)
    small fresh mozzarella
    balls (about 1-inch)
2 tablespoons sliced pitted
    ripe olives

Baked Eyeballs Casserole

START TO FINISH: 50 minutes

Prepping: 15 minutes
Baking: 25 minutes
Standing: 10 minutes

1. Spray a 13×9×2-inch shallow baking dish with the cooking spray.

2. Mix **1½ cups** pasta sauce, ricotta cheese, ½ **cup** Parmesan cheese and pasta in the prepared dish. Spread the remaining pasta sauce over the pasta mixture. Sprinkle with the remaining Parmesan cheese and cover with foil.

3. Bake at 400°F. for 25 minutes or until hot. Arrange the cheese balls randomly over the pasta mixture. Place a sliced olive on each cheese ball. Let stand for 10 minutes before serving.

Makes: 8 servings

Easy Substitution Tip: If fresh mozzarella balls are not available, substitute 1 package (8 ounces) fresh mozzarella. Cut crosswise into thirds. Cut each third in 6 wedges, for triangle-shaped eyes.

Holiday Fun

Bloody Fingers

START TO FINISH: 20 minutes

Prepping: 15 minutes
Baking: 5 minutes

1. Heat the oven to 400°F. Brush the almonds with the food coloring to coat. Set them aside to dry, about 10 minutes.

2. Place the chicken strips on a baking sheet. Brush the narrow end of the chicken strips with egg and press almonds on the egg wash to attach. Bake for 5 minutes or until hot.

3. Pour the pasta sauce in a 2-quart saucepan over medium heat. Cook until it's hot and bubbling, stirring occasionally. Arrange the chicken on a serving platter. Serve with the sauce for dipping.

Makes: 8 servings

Easy Substitution Tip: Substitute frozen fully cooked breaded chicken strips for the refrigerated chicken strips. Increase the bake time to 10 minutes.

24 sliced blanched almonds
   Red liquid **or** paste food
   coloring
2 packages (about 9
   ounces **each**)
   refrigerated fully
   cooked breaded
   chicken strips
   (about 24)
1 egg, slightly beaten
1 jar (1 pound 10 ounces)
   Prego® Traditional
   Pasta Sauce

Holiday Fun

Vegetables and Sides

Crab and Asparagus Risotto

2 tablespoons olive oil
1 medium orange pepper, diced (about 1 cup)
½ cup chopped onion **or** shallots
2 cups **uncooked** Arborio rice (short-grain)
½ cup dry white wine
6 cups Swanson® Chicken Broth (Regular, Natural Goodness™ **or** Certified Organic), heated
½ **pound asparagus or** green beans, trimmed, cut into 1-inch pieces (about 1½ cups)
½ **pound refrigerated** pasteurized crabmeat (about 1½ cups)
¼ **cup grated Parmesan** cheese

START TO FINISH: 35 minutes

Prepping/Cooking: 30 minutes
Standing: 5 minutes

1. Heat the oil in a 4-quart saucepan over medium heat. Add the pepper and onion and cook for 3 minutes or until the vegetables are tender. Add the rice and cook and stir for 2 minutes or until the rice is opaque.

2. Add the wine and cook and stir until it's absorbed. Stir **2 cups** of the hot broth into the rice mixture. Cook and stir until the broth is absorbed, maintaining the rice at a gentle simmer. Continue cooking and adding broth, ½ cup at a time, stirring until it's absorbed after each addition before adding more. Add the asparagus and crabmeat with the last broth addition.

3. Stir the cheese into the risotto. Remove the saucepan from the heat. Cover and let it stand for 5 minutes. Serve the risotto with additional cheese.

Makes: 8 servings

4 teaspoons cornstarch
1¾ cups Swanson®
     Vegetable Broth
     (Regular or Certified
     Organic)
4 medium carrots, sliced
     (about 2 cups)
1 medium onion, chopped
     (about ½ cup)
¾ pound snow peas
1 teaspoon lemon juice

Glazed Snow Peas and Carrots

START TO FINISH: 25 minutes

Prepping: 10 minutes
Cooking: 15 minutes

1. Stir the cornstarch and **1 cup** broth in a small cup. Set the mixture aside.

2. Heat the remaining broth in a 10-inch skillet over medium-high heat to a boil. Add the carrots and onion and reduce the heat to low. Cover and cook for 5 minutes or until the carrots are tender-crisp. Add the snow peas and cook for 2 minutes.

3. Stir the cornstarch mixture and stir it into the skillet. Cook and stir until the mixture boils and thickens. Stir in the lemon juice.

Makes: 8 servings

Vegetables and Sides

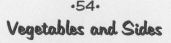

Spaghetti Squash Alfredo

START TO FINISH: 1 hour 10 minutes

Prepping: 10 minutes
Baking/Cooking: 1 hour

1. Pierce squash with fork or skewer in several places. Bake at 350°F. for 50 minutes or until the squash is fork-tender. Cut in half, scoop out and discard seeds. Scrape the flesh with fork to separate the spaghetti-like strands.

2. Stir the soup, water and milk in a 2-quart saucepan. Heat over medium heat to a boil. Stir in the Swiss cheese.

3. Place the hot spaghetti squash in a 2-quart serving bowl. Pour the soup mixture over the squash. Toss to coat. Sprinkle with Parmesan cheese and parsley.

Makes: 5 servings

1 medium spaghetti
    squash (about
    3 pounds)
1 can (10¾ ounces)
    Campbell's®
    Condensed Cream of
    Celery Soup (Regular
    or 98% Fat Free)
¾ cup water
¼ cup milk
1 cup shredded low fat
    Swiss cheese
    (4 ounces)
2 tablespoons grated
    Parmesan cheese
    Chopped fresh parsley
    or chives

Vegetables and Sides

3 cups **uncooked** medium egg noodles

2 cups broccoli flowerets

1 can (10¾ ounces) Campbell's® Condensed Cream of Chicken Soup (Regular or 98% Fat Free)

½ cup sour cream

⅓ cup grated Parmesan cheese

⅛ teaspoon ground black pepper

Broccoli & Noodles Supreme

START TO FINISH: 30 minutes

Prepping: 10 minutes
Cooking: 20 minutes

1. Prepare the noodles according to the package directions in a 4-quart saucepot. Add the broccoli during the last 5 minutes of the cooking time. Drain the noodles and broccoli well in a colander and return them to the saucepot.

2. Stir the soup, sour cream, cheese and black pepper into the noodles and broccoli. Cook and stir over medium heat until hot.

3. Top with additional cheese before serving.

Makes: 5 servings

Vegetables and Sides

Mozzarella Zucchini Skillet

START TO FINISH: 25 minutes

  Prepping: 10 minutes
  Cooking: 15 minutes

1. Heat the oil in a 12-inch skillet over medium-high heat. Add the zucchini, onion and garlic powder and cook until the vegetables are tender-crisp.

2. Stir in the pasta sauce and heat through.

3. Sprinkle with the cheese. Cover and cook until the cheese melts.

Makes: 7 servings

2 tablespoons vegetable oil
5 medium zucchini, sliced (about 7½ cups)
1 medium onion, chopped (about ½ cup)
¼ teaspoon garlic powder **or** 2 cloves garlic, minced
1½ cups Prego® Traditional Pasta Sauce
½ cup shredded mozzarella **or** Cheddar cheese

Corn and Black-Eyed Pea Salad

1 bag (16 ounces) frozen
    whole kernel corn,
    thawed (about 3 cups)
1 can (16 ounces) black-
    eyed peas, rinsed and
    drained
1 large green pepper,
    chopped (about 1 cup)
½ cup chopped red onion
½ cup chopped fresh
    cilantro leaves
1 jar (16 ounces) Pace®
    Chunky Salsa

START TO FINISH: 4 hours 15 minutes

Prepping: 15 minutes
Refrigerating: 4 hours

1. Mix the corn, peas, green pepper, red onion and cilantro in a 2-quart bowl. Stir the salsa into the corn mixture until well coated.

2. Cover and refrigerate the salad for 4 hours.

3. Stir the salad before serving.

Makes: 8 servings

Cooking for a Crowd: Recipe may be doubled.

Make Ahead Tip: Prepare the salad as directed. Cover and refrigerate the salad overnight. Stir the salad before serving.

Vegetables and Sides

Cheddar Broccoli Bake

START TO FINISH: 40 minutes

Prepping: 10 minutes
Baking: 30 minutes

1. Stir the soup, milk, black pepper, broccoli and ⅔ **cup** onions in a 1½-quart casserole and cover.

2. Bake at 350°F. for 25 minutes or until hot. Stir the broccoli mixture.

3. Sprinkle the remaining onions over the broccoli mixture. Bake for 5 minutes more or until the onions are golden.

Makes: 6 servings

1 can (10¾ ounces) Campbell's® Condensed Cheddar Cheese Soup
½ cup milk
  Dash ground black pepper
4 cups cooked broccoli cuts
1 can (2.8 ounces) French fried onions (1⅓ cups)

Vegetables and Sides

Sweet Treats

Southern Pecan Crisps

½ of a 17.3 ounce package Pepperidge Farm® Frozen Puff Pastry Sheets (1 sheet)
½ cup packed brown sugar
⅓ cup pecan halves, chopped
2 tablespoons butter, melted
Confectioners' sugar

START TO FINISH: 1 hour 47 minutes

Thawing: 40 minutes
Prepping: 25 minutes
Baking: 12 minutes
Cooling: 30 minutes

1. Thaw the pastry sheet at room temperature for 40 minutes or until it's easy to handle. Heat the oven to 400°F. Mix the brown sugar and the pecans with the butter in a small bowl.

2. Unfold the pastry sheet on a lightly floured surface. Roll the sheet into a 15×12-inch rectangle. Cut the pastry into (20) 3-inch squares. Press the squares into bottoms of 3-inch muffin-pan cups. Place **1 heaping teaspoon** pecan mixture in the center of **each** cup.

3. Bake for 12 minutes or until golden. Remove the pastry from the pans and cool on a wire rack. Sprinkle the pastries with the confectioners' sugar before serving.

Makes: 20 pastries

½ of a 17.3 ounce package
    Pepperidge Farm®
    Frozen Puff Pastry
    Sheets (1 sheet)
1 egg
1 tablespoon water
2 tablespoons granulated
    sugar
1 tablespoon all-purpose
    flour
¼ teaspoon ground
    cinnamon
2 large Granny Smith
    apples, peeled, cored
    and thinly sliced
2 tablespoons raisins
    Confectioners' sugar
    (optional)

Sweet Treats

Apple Strudel

START TO FINISH: 2 hours 15 minutes

Thawing: 40 minutes
Prepping: 30 minutes
Baking: 35 minutes
Cooling: 30 minutes

1. Thaw the pastry sheet at room temperature for 40 minutes or until it's easy to handle. Heat the oven to 375°F. Lightly grease a baking sheet. Stir the egg and water in a small bowl. Mix the sugar, flour and cinnamon in a medium bowl. Add the apples and raisins and toss to coat.

2. Unfold the pastry sheet on a lightly floured surface. Roll the sheet into a16×12-inch rectangle. With the short side facing you, spoon the apple mixture on the bottom half of the pastry to within 1 inch of the edges. Starting at the short side closest to you, roll up like a jelly roll. Place seam-side down on the baking sheet. Tuck ends under to seal. Brush with the egg mixture. Cut several 2-inch-long slits 2 inches apart on the top.

3. Bake for 35 minutes or until golden. Cool on the baking sheet on a wire rack for 30 minutes. Slice and serve warm. Sprinkle with confectioners' sugar, if desired.

Makes: 6 servings

Sweet Potato Pie

START TO FINISH: 4 hours 45 minutes

Prepping: 15 minutes
Baking: 1 hour
Cooling: 3 hours 30 minutes

1. Heat the oven to 350°F. Put the potatoes in a 3-quart saucepan with enough water to cover them. Heat the potatoes over medium-high heat to a boil. Reduce the heat to low. Cover and cook the potatoes for 10 minutes or until they're fork-tender. Drain the potatoes well in a colander.

2. Place the potatoes in a 3-quart bowl. Add the cream. Beat the potatoes with an electric mixer at medium speed until the potatoes are fluffy and almost smooth. Add the soup, brown sugar, eggs, vanilla, cinnamon and nutmeg. Beat at low speed until the ingredients are mixed. Spoon the potato mixture into the prepared crust and place the pie plate on a baking sheet.

3. Bake for 1 hour or until the center is almost set. Cool the pie in the pan on a wire rack to room temperature.

Makes: 8 servings

Easy Substitution Tip: Substitute **1¾ cups** drained and mashed canned sweet potatoes for fresh mashed sweet potatoes. Beat with cream until fluffy and almost smooth.

3 large sweet potatoes, peeled and cut into cubes (about 3 cups)
¼ cup heavy cream
1 can (10¾ ounces) Campbell's® Condensed Tomato Soup
1 cup packed brown sugar
3 eggs
1 teaspoon vanilla extract
½ teaspoon ground cinnamon
½ teaspoon ground nutmeg
1 (9-inch) unbaked pie crust

Sweet Treats

⅓ cup heavy cream
1 tablespoon orange-
    flavored liqueur **or**
    ½ teaspoon orange
    extract
1 package (about
    12 ounces) white
    chocolate pieces

Suggested Dippers: Assorted Pepperidge Farm® Cookies, whole strawberries, banana chunks, dried pineapple pieces **and/or** fresh pineapple chunks

I'm Dreamy for White Chocolate Fondue

START TO FINISH: 15 minutes

Prepping: 5 minutes
Cooking: 10 minutes

1. Stir the cream, liqueur and chocolate in a 1-quart saucepan. Heat over low heat until the chocolate melts, stirring occasionally.

2. Pour the chocolate mixture into a fondue pot or slow cooker.

3. Serve warm with the *Suggested Dippers.*

Makes 1½ cups

Sweet Treats

Fishy Families

START TO FINISH: 36 minutes 15 seconds

Prepping: 5 minutes
Cooking: 1 minute 15 seconds
Refrigerating: 30 minutes

1. Line a baking sheet with waxed paper and set it aside. Place the chocolate in a microwavable bowl. Microwave on HIGH for 1 minute. Stir. Microwave at 15 second intervals, stirring after each, until the chocolate melts. Stir in the crackers to coat.

2. Scoop up the cracker mixture with a tablespoon and drop onto the prepared baking sheet. Sprinkle with the nonpareils. Repeat with the remaining cracker mixture and nonpareils.

3. Refrigerate for 30 minutes or until the mixture is firm. Store in the refrigerator.

Makes: 1 pound

1 package (12 ounces) semi-sweet chocolate pieces (2 cups)
2½ cups Pepperidge Farm® Pretzel Goldfish® Baked Snack Crackers
1 container (4 ounces) multi-colored nonpareils

16 Reynolds® Foil Baking Cups (2½-inch)
2 packages (4.9 ounces each) Pepperidge Farm® Mini Milano® Distinctive Cookies
2 packages (8 ounces each) cream cheese, softened
½ cup sugar
2 eggs
½ teaspoon vanilla extract

Sweet Treats

Mini Chocolate Cookie Cheesecakes

START TO FINISH: 3 hours 40 minutes

Prepping: 20 minutes
Baking: 20 minutes
Cooling: 1 hour
Refrigerating: 2 hours

1. Heat the oven to 350°F. Put the foil baking cups into 16 (2½-inch) muffin-pan cups or on a baking sheet. Place **2** cookies in the bottom of each cup and set aside. Cut the remaining cookies in half.

2. Beat the cream cheese, sugar, eggs and vanilla in a medium bowl with an electric mixer on medium speed until smooth. Spoon the cheese mixture into the baking cups filling each cup ¾ full. Insert **2** cookie halves, with the cut ends down, into the cheese mixture of each cup.

3. Bake for 20 minutes or until the centers are set. Cool the cheesecakes on a wire rack for 1 hour. Refrigerate the cheesecakes for at least 2 hours before serving.

Makes: 16 servings

Chocolate Cherry Ice Cream Cake

START TO FINISH: 2 hours 25 minutes

Prepping: 10 minutes
Freezing: 2 hours 15 minutes

1. Stand **10** of the cookies on their sides along the edge of a 9-inch springform pan, forming a ring. Coarsely chop the remaining cookies.

2. Spoon the black cherry ice cream into the pan and spread into an even layer. Spoon **1** jar of the chocolate sauce over the ice cream. Sprinkle with the coarsely chopped cookies. Freeze for 15 minutes.

3. Evenly spread the vanilla ice cream over the cookie layer. Pour the remaining chocolate sauce in the center, spreading into a circle to within 1 inch of the edge. Pipe the whipped cream around the top edge. Freeze for 2 hours more or until the mixture is firm. Place the cherries on top of the chocolate sauce just before serving.

Makes: 10 servings

Time-Saving Tip: The ice cream will be easier to spread when it's slightly softened. Let the ice cream sit at room temperature about 10 minutes before spooning onto the crust. Spread gently with a flexible spatula to make an even layer.

1 **package (6 ounces) Pepperidge Farm® Milano® Distinctive Cookies**
1 **container (1.75 quarts) black cherry ice cream**
2 **jars (17 ounces each) chocolate ice cream sauce**
1 **container (1.75 quarts) vanilla ice cream**
  Sweetened whipped cream for garnish
  Frozen pitted dark cherries, thawed for garnish

Beverages

Frosted Citrus Green Tea

2 bottles (16 fluid ounces each) Diet V8 Splash® Tropical Blend Juice **(4 cups), chilled**
4 cups strong brewed green tea*
Fresh mint sprigs (optional)
Lemon slices (optional)

START TO FINISH: 3 hours 30 minutes

Prepping: 2 hours
Freezing/Refrigerating: 1 hour 30 minutes

1. Pour **2 cups** juice into **1** ice cube tray. Freeze for 1 hour 30 minutes or until the mixture is frozen.

2. Mix the remaining juice and tea in an 8-cup measure. Refrigerate for at least 1 hour and 30 minutes.

3. Unmold the cubes from the tray and place 3 to 4 cubes in each of **6** tall glasses. Divide the tea mixture among the glasses. Serve with mint and lemon, if desired.

Makes: 6 servings

*Strong brewed tea: Heat 4 cups of water in a 2-quart saucepan over high heat to a boil. Remove the pan from the heat. Add **8** tea bags and let them steep for 5 minutes. Remove the tea bags.

1 bottle (16 fluid ounces) V8 Splash® Orange Pineapple Juice (2 cups), chilled
1 cup vanilla lowfat yogurt
2 cups frozen whole strawberries or raspberries

Jump Start Smoothie

START TO FINISH: 10 minutes

Prepping: 10 minutes

1. Put the juice, yogurt and strawberries in an electric blender container.

2. Cover and blend until smooth.

3. Serve immediately.

Makes: 4 servings

Lemon Sangria Punch

START TO FINISH: 10 minutes

Prepping: 10 minutes

1. Stir the juice, lemonade and Worcestershire, if desired, lemons, limes and orange in an 8-quart punch bowl.

2. Serve immediately or refrigerate until serving time.

3. Pour over ice-filled tall glasses.

Makes: 20 servings

1 bottle (64 fluid ounces) V8® 100% Vegetable Juice, chilled
1 container (64 fluid ounces) refrigerated lemonade
1 tablespoon Worcestershire sauce (optional)
2 lemons, thinly sliced
2 limes, thinly sliced
1 orange, thinly sliced
Ice cubes

½ cup **V8 Splash® Peach Lemonade or Mango Peach**, chilled
¼ cup **peach nectar**, chilled
1 cup **champagne, sparkling wine or sparkling cider**, chilled

Bellini Splash

START TO FINISH: 5 minutes

Prepping: 5 minutes

1. Stir the juice and nectar in a 1-cup measure.

2. Divide between 2 fluted champagne glasses. Pour in champagne.

3. Serve immediately.

Makes: 2 servings

Cooking for a Crowd: Recipe may be doubled or tripled.

Tropical Freeze

START TO FINISH: 10 minutes

Prepping: 10 minutes

1. Put the juice, sherbet, ice and banana in an electric blender container.

2. Cover and blend until it's smooth.

3. Serve immediately.

Makes: 4 servings

1 bottle (16 fluid ounces) V8 Splash® Tropical Blend Juice (2 cups), chilled
1 pint orange **or** mango sherbet **or** vanilla ice cream
1 cup crushed ice
1 medium banana, sliced

Beverages

2 cans (5.5 fluid ounces **each**) V8® Spicy Hot Vegetable Juice
3 fluid ounces (6 tablespoons) pepper-flavored vodka
Dash chipotle hot pepper sauce (or to taste)
2 cups ice cubes
Seasoned salt (optional)
2 stalks celery

Spicy Mary Martinis

START TO FINISH: 5 minutes

Prepping: 5 minutes

1. Put the juice, vodka, pepper sauce and ice in a cocktail shaker. Cover and shake until blended.

2. Strain into 2 chilled tall glasses rimmed with seasoned salt, if desired.

3. Serve with the celery.

Makes: 2 servings

Russian Witches' Brew

START TO FINISH: 20 minutes

Prepping: 5 minutes
Cooking: 15 minutes

2 bottles (16 fluid ounces each) V8 Splash® Tropical Blend Juice (4 cups)
4 cups strong brewed tea*
11 cinnamon sticks
8 whole cloves

1. Stir the juice, tea, **3** cinnamon sticks and cloves in a 4-quart saucepot. Heat over medium-high heat to a boil. Reduce the heat to medium-low and cook for 10 minutes. Remove the cinnamon sticks and cloves.

2. Place remaining cinnamon sticks in 8 mugs and fill with juice mixture.

3. Serve immediately or keep it warm in the saucepot over very low heat.

Makes: 8 servings

***Strong brewed tea:** Heat 4 cups of water in a 2-quart saucepan over high heat to a boil. Remove the pan from the heat. Add **8** tea bags and let them steep for 5 minutes. Remove the tea bags.

Cooking for a Crowd: Recipe may be doubled or tripled.

Beverages

1 bottle (16 fluid ounces)
    V8® Splash Berry
    Blend Juice (2 cups)
2 fluid ounces (¼ cup) dark
    spiced **or** regular rum
½ teaspoon ground
    cinnamon
¼ teaspoon ground ginger
2 cinnamon sticks

Berry Rum Toddies

START TO FINISH: 10 minutes

Prepping/Cooking: 10 minutes

1. Heat the juice, rum, cinnamon and ginger in a 1-quart saucepan to a boil and cook for 5 minutes, stirring occasionally.

2. Pour the juice mixture into 2 mugs.

3. Serve with the cinnamon sticks. Serve immediately.

Makes: 2 servings

Index